Dogs, Frogs, and Hogs

by Dave Miller, Ph.D.

A.P. "Learn to Read" Series

God made dogs.

See the dogs?

Dogs bark.

Dogs run.

Dogs dig.

Dogs bark, run,
and dig.

Dogs lick.

Dogs like to lick.

Dogs are fun.

God made dogs.

God made frogs.

God made frogs hop.

Hop, frog, hop!

Hop, hop, hop!

Do not hop!

God made frogs.

God made hogs.

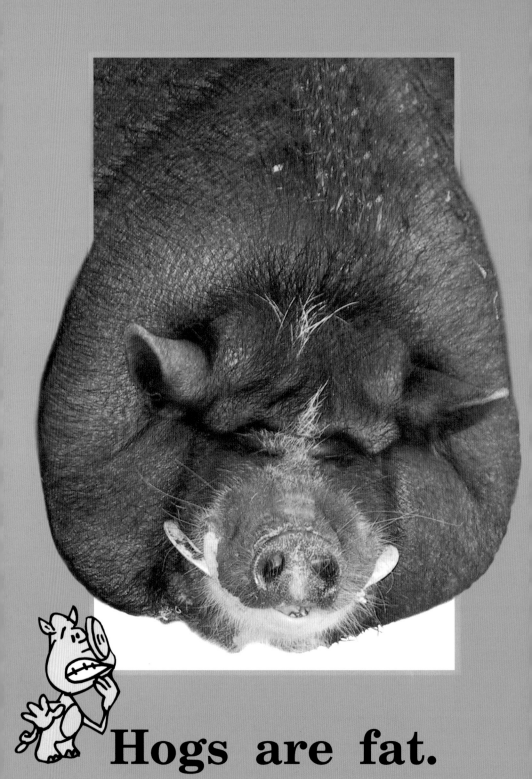

Hogs are fat.

Hogs eat

and eat

and eat.

Hogs get in mud.

Hogs like mud.

God made hogs.

God made dogs, frogs, and hogs.

God made them all.

God made them all
on day six.

God is good!

The "Learn to Read" Series: A Word to Parents

Rationale: To provide books for children (ages 3-6) from Christian homes for the purpose of assisting them in **learning to read** while simultaneously introducing them to the **Creator** and His **creation.**

Difficulty Level

The following listing provides a breakdown of the number and length of words in *Dogs, Frogs, and Hogs* (not counting plurals and duplicates):

Total Number of Words: 33

5 - Two letter words
to, do, in, on, is

20 - Three letter words
God, dog, see, the, run,
dig, and, are, fun, hop,
now, not, hog, fat, eat,
get, mud, all, day, six

8 - Four letter words
made, bark, lick, like,
frog, stop, them, good

**Drawings by
Alanna Hallenbeck, Age 7**